MY JOURNEY

Uncharted Waters

SHEILA HARRY

WESTBOW
PRESS®
A DIVISION OF THOMAS NELSON
& ZONDERVAN

WestBow Press books may be ordered through booksellers or by contacting:

WestBow Press
A Division of Thomas Nelson & Zondervan
1663 Liberty Drive
Bloomington, IN 47403
www.westbowpress.com
1 (866) 928-1240

ISBN: 978-1-9736-6966-1 (sc)
ISBN: 978-1-9736-6968-5 (hc)
ISBN: 978-1-9736-6967-8 (e)

Library of Congress Control Number: 2019909981

Print information available on the last page.

WestBow Press rev. date: 07/24/2019

CONTENTS

INTRODUCTION

H ave you ever found yourself in the middle of a journey you didn't plan? Have you ever found yourself on a journey you didn't want to be on? Well, my journey was neither wanted nor planned.

This is the story of a journey I have recently taken. However, in order to understand the complete impact of this journey, I first need to tell you a little bit about myself. I am currently in my sixties, still working, and, as most folks, have a bit of upheaval in my life. But I have always been a bit stubborn and independent, and tended to have the attitude that, no matter what, I could withstand, endure, and fix whatever was wrong – on my own. Perhaps a good part of this comes from broken relationships, marriages, having family living with me and dependent on me, and then being widowed.

I have been in and out of the church numerous times throughout my life. Although baptized at an early age, and again about ten years later, I am not unfamiliar with scripture and would consider myself to be a Christian person for the most part. However, my self-proclaimed Christianity did not come from a close, personal relationship with God. This would become very apparent as I embarked on this journey.

While I have been relatively healthy throughout most of my life aside from small issues, I have also beaten my body up pretty good physically. I have had several surgeries and broken a few bones. So, I have given little thought to serious – serious - disease. But as you read through this journey, you will see that disease did come along – one more serious than I had ever dreamed of.

CHAPTER 1

"The Beginning"

My household at this time is certainly not "normal" – or at least what I was normally used to. Prior to August 17, 2017, my Mother lived with me. Quite often she would visit her cousin for anywhere from a week to a month at a time. But, for the most part, she was here. On August 17, 2017, while I was working in Georgia, I received a text from my daughter-in-law saying, "My house is on fire." I excused myself from the class I was teaching and went outside the room and called. Sure enough, she was outside watching the fire department working to put out the fire. I dismissed my class early, returned to my hotel to collect Mother and my things and headed home. My family, consisting of my son, daughter-in-law, two grandsons, and a dog would be staying at my house for a bit.

Their insurance company was contacted, and they began looking for a house to rent for an interim period. However, it had to be in the school district, had to be located where the boys could ride the school bus, and must accept the dog. Finding a house for rent that fit the bill proved to be impossible and the decision was made that they would simply stay with me until the house was restored. With all the added activity in the house, Mother made the decision to simply move in with her cousin as this had been discussed between them for a while. So, we settled into the very changed household.

On January 12th, 2018, I woke up with a headache. My head hurt and, as days passed, only became worse. The bad part is that it never stopped – not for a minute. Tylenol and other headache medications simply would not stop it. Finally, on January 23rd, I went to my primary doctor, Dr. Grinder. At that point, the entire right side of my head felt as though it would just explode. I honestly thought it was probably an ear infection. Dr. Grinder looked at my ears with the equipment she had available and saw no issues. There was no ear infection apparent. With this, she put me on an antibiotic, prescribed Lortab, scheduled an MRI and referred me to an ENT. Two days later, I had the MRI performed.

Now, I already had a cruise planned and paid for, so on January 27th I left on the cruise. The cruise was horrible since I had this non-stop headache going on, but I made it through the cruise. On February 6th, I went for my appointment with the ENT., Dr. Colvin. He had read the MRI report. Mind you, this report stated very little fluid and that all sinus cavities were clear. Because of this, he put me on a different antibiotic and referred me to a neurologist, Dr. Newton.

I went by the facility that performed the MRI and picked up a disc to take to Dr. Newton. On February 7th, I went for my appointment with Dr. Newton and explained to him what was going on. I offered the disc but was told that he did not need it because he had the report. He gave no diagnosis, but said we were going to try a medication called Gabapentin and scheduled a return visit on February 23rd. The Gabapentin did absolutely nothing to stop the headache.

When I returned to Dr. Newton on the 23rd I explained that the medication did not help and that nothing had changed. He still gave no diagnosis but stated that we were going to try a different medication called Topamax.

While I had certainly faced difficult situations in the past, I had endured through them. I had never actually experienced any severe depression. However, this constant pain was really getting to me and I found myself sitting in my room, holding my head as though that would keep it from blowing up or stop the pain, and I had the thought, "My 380 would fix this." I think that was probably the real eye-opener for me. I had, regardless of the situation, never had such thoughts.

At that point, I began to have some conversations between

God and myself. With such a long period of pain, I began to realize that my normal "fix it myself" attitude simple wasn't working. I was beginning to realize and admit that I was totally helpless in this situation. This was an attitude and admission to which I was certainly not used to. I had begun reading scripture regularly and praying, ultimately coming to the realization that the only thing I could do on my own was to trust this situation to God. Now, for quite a while, I had been receiving devotional verses each morning via email. Also, on a shelf and with a very dusty cover, I had a prayer devotional book, which I now began reading. I instantly started receiving devotionals each morning reminding me of God's promises and I began using the prayer devotional each morning. With much soul searching, and honest admissions to myself and God, I made the decision to trust my life, my will, and this situation to God and to take this one day at a time. This is when I began really being somewhat at peace with the entire situation despite the constant pain. I was willing to accept whatever the outcome might be.

With the absence of no improvement and no idea what was wrong, I became a bit frustrated and went back to Dr. Grinder on March 12th. She was still clueless but did give me a few pain pills to help with the pain. On March 13th, I went back to Dr. Colvin, the ENT. The girl called me back to take my vitals and my blood pressure was dangerously high. I told her it was probably because of the pain that just would not stop. The audiologist was standing there and took me to her office to look at a couple of things. When she checked the pressure in my ears, it was way off the mark of where it should be. This was relayed to Dr. Colvin who then decided to scope my head. When he did this, he found that there was, in fact, quite a bit of fluid behind the ears, particularly on that right side. Apparently either the eustachian tube was blocked or collapsed. Dr. Colvin opened the right ear that day – not pleasant – but the fluid gushed out and the extreme pressure pain immediately went away. However, I still had a headache and my scalp just felt like it was burning and stinging. One week later, on March 20th, Dr. Colvin opened the left ear. Again, the head felt a bit better, but not much.

On April 3rd, I returned to the neurologist for my appointment and asked him very directly what was wrong. He admitted that he had no idea. That was the end of my appointments with him.

CHAPTER 2

"The Diagnosis"

I continued to see Dr. Colvin, who continued to attempt to determine what was causing the headache. Between April 3rd and April 17th, Dr. Colvin did a CT scan on my head in his office. He discovered that the Sphenoid Nasal cavity was full of fluid and scheduled surgery on April 18th to drain that cavity. When I returned to Dr. Colvin for my post op visit on April 24th, he scheduled another MRI from a different facility. They began the MRI on April 26th and completed it on May 1st. On May 2nd, while in Georgia working, I got a call from the ENT's office stating that they had the results and that he wanted me in his office on the 3rd. So, on May 3rd, Dr. Colvin told me that the MRI clearly showed that there was "something" there. However, he could not clearly see what the "something" was. He scheduled surgery on May14th to explore exactly what was showing on the MRI.

On May 14th, they did the surgery, verifying what the MRI was showing, and performed biopsies. On the 16th the ENT's office called and wanted me to come in on the 17th. I went to my ENT's office on the 17th, taking my son with me. When the doctor came in, he told me that there was, in fact, a tumor. I brought my son back so that he could hear the explanation. Dr. Colvin explained that the tumor did not have a clearly defined shape but was instead kind of flat and diffused. He also explained that the biopsies revealed that it was, in fact, squamous cell carcinoma. So, there was the big "C" word – the one nobody wants to hear.

We discussed the location, wedged in between the nasopharynx, main optic nerve and the brain stem. This would, of course, mean no surgery. He explained in general what this meant and what the treatment would be. I was then told that my first step would be to decide where I wanted to receive treatment. I asked if I could have a couple of days and he said that would be fine, just not to wait like a month to decide.

I came home and did a good bit of research online as to the available technologies at both UAB Medical Center and Grandview Medical Center. I also put quite a bit of time into prayer over the decision. Dr. Colvin is associated with Grandview Medical Center so, of course, if I decided on a different facility, I would have to make an appointment with an ENT at that facility, although Dr. Colvin would still monitor the situation. I came to a decision on May 18th, led by a couple of things. First, I felt it would waste time to have to see another ENT who would probably want to do some of their own tests. Secondly, Grandview Medical Center had the same technologies available as other facilities in the area, plus there were just about to open a brand-new Comprehensive Cancer Center of their own. Most important, through prayer and conversations with God, I felt that He was leading me to simply stay with my ENT and his facility. So, on the 18th, I called and told his office that I decided to proceed with them.

On Monday, May 21st, my ENT called me, and I discussed with him the fact that I had decided to continue treatment with his facility. His office then made me an appointment with my oncologist, Dr. Harvey, who is a very experienced oncologist. The appointment was made for the next day, May 22nd. This would begin my journey of finding out exactly what this diagnosis meant for me and what the treatment options were.

On the 22nd, I went to the appointment with Dr. Harvey. He explained the typical treatments and we discussed my general health. Since I was otherwise healthy, he recommended proceeding with chemotherapy and radiation treatments simultaneously. He ordered a PET scan to better pinpoint the cancer location and stated that, unless the PET scan showed something unexpected, we would begin chemo treatments on Thursday, May 31st. At this point, he stated that he would use oral chemo and I would be able to do that at home, taking the chemo medication orally for 14 days and then have a 3-week break. I would then, for the second round, take the oral medication for another 14 days. We would also be doing radiation treatment simultaneously with the chemotherapy. The plan was to order another PET scan at the end of round 2 of the chemo to track progress. He was optimistic that this PET scan would be clear.

At this time, I still had the headaches and therefore, not feeling very well most of the time. However, I will still be receiving very assuring devotions each morning and can honestly say that I felt a kind of peace about this whole situation. My feeling was complete confidence that God could and would handle this and I was wiling to accept that He would do so on His own timetable. A good example of the assurances I had been receiving occurred at 4:45 AM on May 27th. I was sitting in my chair by the bed contemplating looking at the PET scan images myself to see if I could tell if the cancerous cells were in other places as well. My cell phone beeped, indicating that an email had come in. I looked to see what it was, and it was a devotional quoting Philippians 4:6.

"Don't worry about anything; instead, pray about
everything. Tell God what you need, and thank
him for all he has done." Philippians 4:6

In other words, don't worry about the PET scan disc, just go back
to bed and sleep and let God worry about the PET scan. I have
to say that I do not know if I could have made it through all of
this had my attitude not been turned more towards trusting God
and a whole bunch less of trying to trust my own self to "fix"
things. This has really engrained in me how helpless I am - how
helpless we all are without God. Later in the day, however, I
became nauseous and could not even keep down a sip of Sprite or
bite of saltine crackers. This lasted throughout the rest of the day
on Sunday, the 27th as well as through the day on Monday and
through the night. This also meant that I could not keep down
any pain meds and my head was having a field day. On Tuesday
I called Dr. Harvey's office and they called in a prescription for
a medication called Zofran for the nausea. Of course, this, and
the lack of information back from the PET scan would delay the
start of treatment. I was hoping to receive this information on
Wednesday morning. With the help of the Zofran, I was able to

keep down light food and some pain medication. However, having not received any information from the PET scan, I waited until after noon and called the doctor's office only to find that they were closed. All I can do at this point is to look to my heavenly Father for comfort.

On Thursday, May 31ˢᵗ, I received the call I had been waiting on with information from the PET scan. Unfortunately, the first assumption that there was no lymph node involvement was incorrect. It also showed that the tumor was much larger than they first thought. The good news was that the lymph nodes had apparently done their job and stopped the spread of the cancer cells there. Of course, this changed the game plan for treatment. Due to the tumor being much larger and the lymph node involvement, the doctor decided that I should have surgery to have a port inserted and would receive a chemo treatment, with a pump that would continue to deliver a low dose of chemo for five days. I would then have a 21-day break, and then have a second treatment with a pump to deliver a low dose for another 5 days. We would then finish up with three to four weeks of radiation treatments. Dr. Harvey was still optimistic about the prognosis. He ordered nausea patches which I would put on 24 hours prior to the chemo treatment.

Of course, I found all this to be disappointing, but I reminded myself that God had this. He did not promise a trouble-free life but only that He would walk through the trials with us. Again, I simply must trust this to Him.

And so, On June 5th, I had to report to the hospital early in the morning for the surgery to implant the port. Once that was completed, I went to Dr. Harvey's office for the first round of chemotherapy treatment. Again, just a couple of days ago, my devotional verse was quoting Exodus 14:14.

"The Lord himself will fight for you. Just stay calm."

This was very encouraging. I can just trust Him and stay calm and let Him fight this battle for me.

CHAPTER 3

"Chemo"

On June 5th, Dr. Harvey began treatment. The day started with me reporting to the hospital early in the morning for minor outpatient surgery to place a port in my chest. This procedure went well with no complications. After this procedure was completed and I was in recovery for a bit, then I was taken for my first chemo treatment. I must admit I had no idea how long a chemo treatment would take! First, they flush the port line with saline, followed by a small bag of anti-nausea medication. Then they hang a bag of chemo medication that must drip through. This is followed by yet another bag of anti-nausea medication. To my surprise, once this was completed, there was another bag of chemo medication. All of this is administered through the port in my chest. Once all the drugs were administered through the IV, they pushed a small vial of saline to clear the line. We had one small glitch – when the nurse tried to disconnect the line from the port, it was simply "frozen" and ultimately broke. She had to remove the line all the way back to the port and re-install a new line. The nurse walked me through this entire procedure in case I ever needed to do it myself. This way, I would be able to disconnect the pump myself when it ran out after the five (5) days. The pump was then hooked up so that it could intermittently continue to deliver a low dose for the next five days. The pump hangs around my neck and is a bit heavy. I am scheduled to return to the oncologist on Monday so that a Neulasta patch can be administered. Admittedly, this part of the treatment went very well with little to no discomfort. I had thought that a big plate of enchiladas sounded great for dinner but opted for a more sensible dinner of chicken noodle soup and crackers, followed by a bowl of chocolate ice cream. In my defense of the ice cream, they have suggested I would suffer a weight loss of 30 to 40 pounds and recommended a high calorie diet. I fell asleep around 8 PM and slept until 7:30 AM the next morning. So far, I feel fine – no headache of any type.

The following Thursday, I began feeling sick. I was so nauseated that I could not keep any food or even fluids on my stomach. The doctor was called and called in some anti-nausea medication, but it simply did not work. The nausea continued and by Sunday, I was dehydrated. My son carried me to the hospital. They worked to control both nausea and diarrhea, which developed after I was admitted to the hospital. To complicate matters, my blood work came back showing my white blood cell count at 1.1 and I was told that they like for cancer patients to maintain a white blood cell count of at least 4. You cannot enter my room without a mask.

They also began giving me injections in my stomach to promote white blood cell production.

On Tuesday, it appeared that my white blood cell count was responding to the medication and attempting to rebound. Apparently, I am now sufficiently hydrated as they have discontinued the IV drip. However, around noon, I was informed that a stool culture indicated that I showed positive for CDEF bacteria, which is highly contagious. Since this bacterium is passed via contact, you now must not only don the mask, but also gloves and a sterile gown to enter my room. This is also apparently the reason for the diarrhea, which is still not under control. They are, however, starting a new oral antibiotic today.

It is now Wednesday, and I am still fighting the CDEF and the resulting diarrhea. I also had an MRI this afternoon. The MRI showed that the tumor has attached to or invaded a bone close to the base of my skull. This apparently means that we will have to go ahead and begin radiation and do chemo and radiation simultaneously. I was told that, in the meantime, I would be in a neck brace to prevent any possible inadvertent neck injury which would allow this to get into the spinal cord. I should learn more tomorrow when meeting with my oncologist and the radiology department. I just must remember, at this point, that God's got this, and He will walk through it with me. I cannot fix this myself – so I must trust it to Him.

So, today I met with Dr. Harvey again and got some clarification. The tumor has, in fact, invaded the bone at the base of my skull. Therefore, the game plan of chemo followed by radiation has been changed. I am to begin having radiation on Monday. This will be a daily process, Monday through Friday, for whatever period of time they deem necessary. I may also be receiving chemo along the way. Dr. Harvey assured me that this would be a low enough dosage that there would be no nausea or low white blood cell counts. The best news was that I would be discharged from the hospital on Friday, on the condition that my white blood cell count goes up to 3 points. Now, this has certainly not been a smooth journey so far. But then, God never promised us a smooth journey. What He did promise is that He would walk the journey with us. I have made the choice to trust this, as well as the rest of my life, to Him and I know that He's got this handled. I also know that He is walking through this journey by my side.

"When you go through deep waters, I will be with you.

When you go through rivers of difficulty, you will not drown.

When you walk through the fire of oppression, you will not be

burned up; the flames will not consume you." Isaiah 43:2

It is time for a huge praise report. My white blood cell count had previously gone up to 3 points on occasion but would then fall back. Blood was drawn about 3:00 a.m. on Friday morning and I was later told that I would be going home. The white blood cell count had mysteriously jumped to 8 points. The nurses seemed amazed as did the doctor. Now that was God showing up and showing out for sure. By Friday afternoon I was home, able to eat a good meal and was not sick or in pain.

On the following Sunday, I felt pretty good. I emptied the dishwasher, cleaned the kitchen, did some light vacuuming, and then had company for a bit. Once company was gone, I cleaned the tub and took a good hot bath and got hair washed. I had mistakenly thought this would be invigorating. I had no concept of how much of an energy drain a bath would be! Ran a couple of errands after resting a bit - my first time out driving alone. Then, tonight we all went to Outback to treat my son for Father's Day.

My appetite is getting better as food seems to slowly return to a normal taste. Although I feel absolutely "useless" at this point, I am proud of what I accomplished today and grateful that God is restoring my energy. I think the better my energy level going into the radiation now, the better off I will be. It is my understanding that fatigue will be the side effect of the radiation.

CHAPTER 4

"Radiation Preparation"

Monday, June 18th was my first appointment with my radiology oncologist, Dr. De Los Santos. She had reviewed all the reports and we sat down and talked about the situation. She explained that what I had was classified as Nasopharyngeal cancer, which she said is not common. She also stated that the reports indicated that it is at Stage Three (3). When I asked for a prognosis, she told me that the 5-year survival rate was 70%.

Next, we discussed the treatment plan. She stated that they were going to continue with the platinum-based chemotherapy concurrently with the radiation treatments. She said there would be three rounds of chemotherapy and thirty-three radiation treatments. The radiation treatments would be done daily Monday through Friday. She explained all the side effects that I could expect and what they would do to manage them, as well as the pain management plan they would have in place.

So, after this somewhat "scary" conversation, she said they were going to spray the nasal cavities with lidocaine so that she could scope my head and put eyes on the tumor. From the length of that scope, I began wondering if she was a gastroenterologist in disguise. She explored for what seemed like forever. Then removing the scope, she stated that she had gone in expecting to find a tumor mass somewhat protruding downward. But she said while shaking her head, it is absolutely miniscule. She repeated this three times and talked about how shocked she was. She then said she was going to get the latest MRI images from the hospital and review them herself. Apparently, that first round of chemo had drastically shrank the tumor. However, we are proceeding. We will have a planning session next Monday, June 25th to work out all the details and will then begin treatment on July 9th. This means I will be able to go on our yearly vacation trip to the beach with the kids. Great news!!

I did feel good today though – I actually worked half a day. We went out to dinner and the food tasted really good. So – folks – once again God has not only shown up but shown out as well!! My next step was to go to UAB Dental on Tuesday, June 19th. They were to do an assessment on the six (6) teeth I have remaining on the bottom. The dentist recommended having them removed. When I refused, she brought in the head of the clinic who explained that, even though the bone structure underneath those teeth are good at this point, that the radiation could damage the bones. He said that in any case, it would take the bones one year to heal and that if anything happened to one of the teeth during that time and it had to be removed, that we could have some real problems. I still refused. They are sending me to a prosthodontist at Kirklin Clinic, Dr. Kase, who will make the special mouthpiece I will have to wear during radiation treatments. They are going to go ahead and make a fluoride tray for me to use on those teeth daily. However, it won't be ready until Friday.

Even with the good reports I have gotten so far, it is still sometimes so difficult to avoid the negative thoughts that Satan tires to interject. My daughter-in-law and I talked about this subject this morning and how we needed to simply pray for strength to ward those thoughts off. At that time, we checked our daily devotional. It was Isaiah 40:31.

> *"When you go through deep waters, I will be with you.*
> *When you go through rivers of difficulty, you will not drown.*
> *When you walk through the fire of oppression, you will*
> *not be burned up; the flames will not consume you."*
> *Isaiah 41:31*

Isn't it amazing how the Father gives us exactly what we need when we need it? Now, He may not always give us that we might "think" we need or what we ask for – but He always gives us what we need if we simply trust in Him.

It is Thursday morning, June 21st and I woke up with my mind a bit troubled this morning. The left side of my neck is very sore. This is the first really valid sign or indication that perhaps the cancer cells have, in fact, invaded some of the lymph nodes. It is so very easy to let Satan enter doubts and worries into our minds. So, I started looking at some of my "go to" scriptures. Romans 8:28 says:

> *"And we know that God causes everything to work*
> *together[a] for the good of those who love God and*
> *are called according to his purpose for them."*

This is certainly one of my favorite reassuring verses. I then went to Dr. Charles Stanley's devotional for today. As usual, since we are given what we need when we need it, today's devotional hit the nail on the head. In this devotional, Dr. Stanley stated: "When our hearts and minds are agitated because of turbulent events, it's hard not to stare at circumstances in horror or confusion. But we must decide to believe what the Bible says about God's character, activity, and purposes. That choice forces our attention off the storm and onto the One responsible for ushering us safely through. In His presence, fears dwindle and doubts dissolve; peace and a sense of oneness with the Lord will take their place. Our responsibility is to keep our eyes on God and trust His Holy Spirit to provide strength, wisdom, and courage." So, I again made the conscious decision to simply trust God with this. Even though I cannot see the big picture or know how all of this will turn out, I can rest on His promise to walk through this with me and work all things for good.

The appointment with Dr. Kase today went well. After reviewing my "head and neck" sheet which shows exactly where the radiation would be concentrated, he concurred with my decision not to have the teeth pulled. I go back to him on Tuesday to pick up the device.

It is Saturday, June 23rd. I came downstairs to make and have my coffee as usual. Since it is the weekend, everyone is home. I was sitting at my desk and my head was itching. When I reached up to scratch it, I came away with a massive handful of hair. I ran my hand through my hair a couple more times with the same result. I called the shop where I usually have my hair done to see if the lady that does it was working, talked to her on the phone and told her what was happening, and she told me to come on over. So, finished coffee, got dressed and headed to Great Clips. I asked her if the hair could be saved and she ran her hands through it and said that it could not. I asked her what I should do, since I had to idea. She explained that I had a couple of options. I could do an actual "razor" shave or a "buzz cut" with the clippers. When I asked which was best, she explained that a little hair might try to grow back but it would be in patches. So, I decided on the "buzz cut" and just like that my hair was gone. When I got home, my oldest grandson, AJ, brought me his ball cap to wear.

It is June 24th and a beautiful Sunday morning. I slept through the night for the first time in a very long time. I was happy to have gotten a good solid eight hours of uninterrupted sleep. My fluid is down this morning, so hopefully I am finally getting rid of that. I had a restful day yesterday although I did get out and met my BF for a short Wally World trip and dinner. I can tell that my energy level is slowly climbing again. I did walk across the street and visit with a lovely neighbor of mine, Miss Malinda. She has brought me gorgeous flowers a couple of times and they really brighten my day. She also gave me a ball cap so now I have a collection going. I want to say thanks to the person, who shall remain anonymous, that offered to also shave their head in support. (Not that their head hasn't been shaved for years already!) My devotional this morning from Dr. Stanley was based on Romans 5:1-5. Romans 5:1-2 talks about having peace because of what Jesus Christ did for us.

"Therefore, since we have been made right in God's sight by faith, we have peace[a] with God because of what Jesus Christ our Lord has done for us. Because of our faith, Christ has brought us into this place of undeserved privilege where we now stand, and we confidently and joyfully look forward to sharing God's glory."

Romans 5:3-5 states,

"We can rejoice, too, when we run into problems and trials, for we know that they help us develop endurance. And endurance develops strength of character, and character strengthens our confident hope of salvation. And this hope will not lead to disappointment. For we know how dearly God loves us, because he has given us the Holy Spirit to fill our hearts with his love."

The devotionals I receive are so encouraging that reminds me that God gives us what we need when we need it.

It is early Tuesday morning. I had a pretty good day yesterday.

Of course, it was back to work for me as the Summer B semester started. I could tell that my energy level is slowly climbing. Everyone's prayers and support through this journey so far are greatly appreciated. I have certainly learned two important lessons:

1. that without God I am totally helpless; and
2. I must simply put my faith in Him and trust my life to Him.

I know that He is walking through this journey with me. I read the daily devotional from Dr Charles Stanley this morning and thought about how very true it was. The scripture reference is Matthew 14:22-33. It is the story of how the disciples were out on stormy waters in a boat when Jesus came walking toward them. Peter stepped out of the boat and began walking on the water toward Jesus. Then he let fear of the stormy waters cause doubt and began to sink

I have those days and times. I know God has this but then I take my focus off Him and Satan takes the opportunity to interject negative thoughts in my mind trying to shake that faith and trust. Last night by the time I made it to bed I had a slight headache. So, Satan took that opportunity to start interjecting those negative thoughts: what if the tumor is growing again? What if it is now spreading? As a result, I did not have the restful night that I have been having recently. Instead only a very few hours' sleep interrupted several times by me waking up. So, I again this morning have to simply make that conscious choice to simply trust this to God. He's got this. A couple of doctor appointments today but nothing major. I will see my primary just to kind of check in and then to the specialist who is making the mouthpiece. Hopefully it will be ready today so that the planning meeting and simulation can proceed as scheduled for tomorrow afternoon.

The appointment with my primary went well. She discontinued the blood pressure medication she had prescribed for the high blood pressure after the headaches started since the blood pressure has come back to normal now that the headaches have stopped. The other appointment went well also as the mouthpiece was ready and fit great.

Today is Wednesday, June 27th and I went back to Radiology Oncology today to meet with Dr. De Los Santos, who we all simply call Dr. "D". For now, there is so much difference in what the original PET scan showed (regarding the tumor) and what she saw when she scoped my head last week, they had to do new scans today. However, we will start radiation treatment on Monday, July 9th. I will have another chemo treatment that morning and then go downstairs to have my first radiation treatment. They did go ahead and make my "mask" today and did a radiation simulation. This was very scary for me and I remembered a verse that actually became my "go to" scripture throughout the radiation treatments. Isaiah 41:10 states:

"Don't be afraid, for I am with you.
Don't be discouraged, for I am your God.
I will strengthen you and help you.
I will hold you up with my victorious right hand."

All of that went well. Once the new scans are back, we will again discuss the treatment details regarding how much chemo I will have and how many radiation treatments. I am feeling good and am having no head pain at all. I am going to drive over to Georgia tomorrow to sit down with my boss and explain the situation just to bring him up to speed. A friend is going with me although I don't anticipate any problems driving over there and back. I just thank the Lord for the progress we have made so far and rest in the knowledge that He has this. I constantly rely on my "go to" scripture.

It is Friday, June 29th. I did go to Georgia yesterday and met with my boss as I felt that I needed to bring him up to date in person. I was hoping to have actual details to give him, which I did not. I simply told him what we had discussed in general – 3 more chemo treatments and 33 radiation treatments. Of course, if the treatment plan remains the same, radiation treatments won't be over until August 22nd and the semester begins on August 15th. I explained to him that I had a game plan in place and that if the treatment plan remained the same, I would simply begin the one class that is not 100% online virtually. He had no problem with that. Today, I had to take the original PET scan images to Grandview, get an oil change for the car, clean the car out and get it washed. It was a busy day, but I am still feeling good. Now, I must get packed for the beach vacation with the family and then just relax. I am certainly looking forward to it. I figure this may be my last "normal" week for a couple of months or more, so I plan to enjoy it.

It is now Saturday night, June 30th, and I am sitting on the balcony of this beautiful condo listening to the waves. It has been a very hectic day and I am tired but still pain free and feeling pretty good. A big shout out of praise and thanks to my Heavenly Father for this treatment free week to enjoy in this wonderful setting and with my son, daughter-in-law and grandsons before we begin another round of chemo and radiation treatments on July 9th.

This thought process has been on my mind and heart for several days. And I have been as guilty of this in the past as much as anyone else. Sometimes we tend to treat God like a lamp with a genie. We polish our lamp and sit it on a shelf all bright and shiny for everyone else to see. However, that is all we do. Until something goes wrong. Then when adversity comes our way we run and grab our lamp and rub it waiting for God the genie to pop out so that we can tell Him what we want Him to do - how we want Him to fix this. Once the adversity is resolved we dust our lamp off and sit it back on the shelf. And it sits there for everyone to see - until the next time.

My current journey has taught me one thing loud and clear. God is NOT a genie in a lamp. My faith is NOT something to be put on display for others to see but not actually used except in times of adversity. I am NOT in control. If I think that I can summon God at my neck and call and direct Him what to accomplish and how them am I not saying that I am greater and more powerful than He? Guess what? I am NOT God and I am totally helpless without Him.

This cancer has certainly shown me that I am totally helpless without Him. It will take a conscious effort on my part to begin every day with Him, to start each day making the choice to trust my life, will and problems to Him and to be ready to accept whatever His will is. And while I am sure I will struggle with this from time to time I am equally as sure that I will no longer treat Him like a genie in a shiny lamp.

It is Tuesday night. I have had a good vacation so far. One bit of disappointment is that my headache is back. Tylenol helps but is not quite stopping it. Hopefully it will be a bit better by tomorrow. I am not going to get discouraged because I know God has this. This coming Monday they will start a second round of chemo and start radiation so maybe it will be better soon.

It is Thursday morning. The fireworks were great. They were really loud, so head didn't appreciate them so much but made it through. The headache pain in the right temple is back full force. Thankfully the scalp pain that was being caused by the tumor pressing on nerves to the scalp is not back though, so I know it hasn't returned to the size it was before

God has blessed me so much already in this process. The amount of shrinkage in the tumor with the first round of chemo, the ease of getting all the necessary devices made for radiation, the speed with which I was able to bounce back from chemo and so many other things. All the credit for these things belongs to Him. I cannot take credit for any of them. He has really shown up during this. Meds are controlling the headache though for the most part and I feel certain that once we begin treatments again on Monday that it will improve.

It is Saturday morning but for us it is still Friday night. We got home from Orange beach about an hour ago. We typically drive back through at night to avoid the traffic.

My head has not gotten any better. As a matter of fact, it is a bit worse. It had always been worse late in the evening and at night, so I was concerned about the drive. I made it almost to Montgomery and we did have to stop and let Andy drive my car on in. I had taken Tylenol - more than I guess I should have but just couldn't get the head calmed down. Anyway, we made it in safely and I will take some additional medication and try to get some sleep. Regardless of the head pain coming back I thank God for this past week with the family.

CHAPTER 5

"Treatments Begin"

It is Monday morning, and this is a short update. I am at Grandview receiving my second chemo treatment. These take about 4 hours. Once done here I have to see my oncologist and then downstairs for my first radiation treatment. I will try to update everyone this evening at some point. I have a class scheduled for 8 pm, assuming I'm able to conduct the class.

Well, it is Tuesday afternoon. I have not had a good day today. I woke up nauseated this morning. It could be the chemo, or it could be the Percocet I took for my head last night. It could just be a combo of the two. Anyway, I took a Phenergan for the nausea and it put me in bed and I am still not feeling well. I went for first radiation treatment. It was not bad at all, except for the already not feeling well. So, I am about to take me back to bed to rest a bit more.

Okay. It is now Monday night. It was a long day today. I arrived at Grandview at 10:25. By the time they got the access line into the port and the lab work done, and they got the first bag hung, it was 11. We did not finish until 4 pm. Then, I met with both Dr. De La Santos (radiology oncology doctor) and Dr. Harvey (oncologist). They did not do a radiation treatment today. Dr. "D" has had the physicists do Five (5) simulations and she stated that she still was not satisfied with the latest one. She has them doing it again. I am scheduled for 3:30 pm tomorrow afternoon assuming she is satisfied with the simulation. Apparently, and my understanding is, this is where they plan specifically where the radiation beams will be aimed and the exact point (intersection of beams) at which the radiation will be delivered.

The reason this is being such an issue is that this tumor is not a nice, neatly shaped tumor. It seems to be a bit elusive and oddly shaped or lacking any definitive shape. It is hard to explain without graphics, but it is located at the back of the sphenoid cavity. There are sinus cavities situated right behind your eyes and the sphenoid cavity sits behind these cavities. This also means that it is right in front of the brain stem. The pituitary gland is also in close proximity as is the Optic nerve. In short, this is a very delicate area in which to be working. Dr. "D"'s dissatisfaction with the latest simulation was that it took the beam only 5 mm away from the brain stem, which she was uncomfortable with. I would rather them take their time and map out the very safest route possible for these radiation beams. Having some working knowledge of biology, I fully realize that this is a tough spot. It appears that, in the absence of a clean PET scan, I will have 3 more rounds of chemo and we are still looking at 33 radiation treatments.

I have put this in God's hands and His will be done. I am hoping and praying that the chemo will shrink or damage this tumor enough that it will be a bit safer to radiate. As for how I am feeling, right now I feel pretty good. The head pain is still here, but Dr. Harvey provided meds for that. We have, on board, the nausea meds that we KNOW are effective with me, so I am hoping this time goes much better. The dosage is NOT as strong as round one either. I still have not gained any weight as they had hoped that I would prior to radiation, even though I am eating very high calorie items and plenty of it, i.e. 3 yeast rolls at O'Charley's tonight! Thanks to all who are sending prayers. Prayer is very powerful. But, praise God for His being with me so far in this journey.

Well, it is Friday night and I am just now getting home from yet another stay in the hospital. Of course, they did chemo on Monday and were able to do radiation on Tuesday, but by Wednesday, I was so nauseated from the chemo that they could not do the radiation. When I was still sick on Thursday, they admitted me to the hospital. I feel much better, but then they have been running Phenergan and fluids via IV. So that has kept the nausea down. Dr.

Harvey came in this morning and came back this afternoon and said he would let me come home. This will give me a couple of days to make sure that I can manage the nausea with oral medications so that we can get started on the radiation again on Monday. Dr. "D" says this tumor is being very aggressive in trying to invade the brain stem and we must get the radiation treatments done, even if we have to completely stop chemo. So, I am home and feel decent. I will be working on controlling everything with the oral meds the next couple of days.

It has been a pretty good day. I have had no nausea today, so maybe that is over with from this round of chemo. There, for certain, will not be any more chemo for the next 3 weeks and supposedly will not be any more 3-week doses at all. The doctors feel the radiation is much more important at this point. I have been able to be up and around today - even went out with Jason for a bit. I do notice that, even though it is not yet 7 pm, I am getting tired. So, it is about time to retire to my room and rest. I did get to be out around the pool area for a while today and Jason got the new planters set out and got one of the umbrellas out to see how it was all going to look together. My pool area is kind of my sanctuary even if just to sit and look around and watch the water. Of course, we are still working on pool issues, but it is coming along.

Thank you to everyone for the prayers. Prayer holds an awful lot of power. And, after all, this is all in His hands and will go according to His will. He doesn't promise a smooth path - only that He will walk it with us.

Unfortunately, today has not been nearly as good as yesterday. I have just had no energy today. My stomach hasn't felt quite right either. I sat outside for a while and watched Andy and Brad work on the pool. But it was so hot I couldn't stay out there long. I did end up taking a Phenergan to help settle stomach. It helps but seems to make me really tired. Hopefully I will feel much better tomorrow.

Ok. Wednesday afternoon update. Radiation went off without a hitch. I have felt much better today. Dr D talked to me after treatment. I was a little disappointed that they don't do the types of scans where you can track the actual progress. Dr D says what we really go by at this point is how I feel. Like whether there is still pain in the back of the head or in the temple. I am happy to say that there is not. She says that means it is working. Prognosis is that I should feel well the rest of this week and possibly next week as well before the side effects of the radiation really start kicking in. I am glad to report that I felt well enough to leave the doctor's office and go meet some friends and spend some time at Mom's Basement Bar. It felt good to be out for a bit just enjoying good conversation with friends, as well as some pizza rolls. Again, God has this. He walks with us through these valleys and strengthens us along the way. Thank you, Lord.

Today was a good day. I volunteered as an usher for the Red mountain Theater today and got to watch Mama Mia. The play was great. I didn't have quite as much energy today - or maybe was still a little tired from yesterday. Either way, that one adventure was all I could handle today.

The issue with the thick mucus is becoming a real inconvenience. Peppermint candy seems to help as does drinking lemonade. I am also doing the salt/soda gargle thing.

It is Saturday morning and time for an update. For the most part, things are still good, and the doctor says I can expect maybe one more week of feeling fairly good. Wednesday night, after the update, I just had a bad night in that I could never fall asleep - not even the "nod off" and miss 10 minutes of the best part of the movie kind of night. Thursday, of course, was a workday so I didn't get to nap during the day then. Radiation went well that afternoon but after I got home and ate, I really crashed. I fell asleep early and slept for hours and hours. As a result, I didn't really talk to anyone or post any kind of update. Friday (yesterday) was the busiest day I have attempted in quite a while. I had some work to finish early and my radiation had been rescheduled to 10:15 am at my request. So, radiation went well and then up to the doctor's office for lab work. Once this was done, I got back home and got a couple of things done before leaving again at 12:30. I met a friend at the movies, and we watched the 1:15 showing of the new Mama Mia movie. Afterward, another friend met up with us and we went to Saw's Juke Joint for a late lunch. This was my first trip there and the food did not disappoint. After a leisurely meal and talking, we decided to go to the Crestwood Pharmacy. They have the old fashioned "soda fountain". We were joined by a couple of others and all enjoyed shakes/ice cream. Once home again - which was between 6:30 and 7:00 p.m., it was time to relax. I was very tired, but the day was a really fun day. Thank God for the energy to enjoy the day. But, again, I did not take the time to update. Today, I have one more adventure planned - but not nearly as adventurous as yesterday. I will be volunteering as an usher (with a friend of mine) at the Red Mountain Theater for the 2:00 pm play which just happens to be the new Mama Mia. I am excited to get to contrast the movie with the on-stage rendition. This should be fun. I think, though, that is all I will plan for today. Time to rest up. One negative is that the mucus is really thickening so it is time to go on Mucinex as well as do the salt/baking soda gargles. I may have to investigate either a larger cool mist humidifier for the bedroom or at least an additional one. The mucus is now so thick that it tends to want to clog the throat. Thankfully, there is not yet a lot of throat soreness though. My morning coffee really helps this as well.

I can tell you that, if nothing breaks or bends, I believe I will get to be at church in person tomorrow. I really miss that. I am ever thankful that my church, Church of the Highlands, has the online campus. This has allowed me to still be able to hear the awesome music and the word from Pastor Chris - it is such a blessing. But there really is not quite anything like being there in person. I am so thankful that the Lord is walking through this valley with me, encouraging and lifting me up. I could not do this without Him.

It is about noon time on Monday. I did not get to make it to church in person yesterday. It was very disappointing. The whole thick mucus thing is getting difficult to deal with - especially in the mornings. I have started on the Mucinex and hopefully this will help. So far, the gargle has not made much difference. I will talk to them today about using a saline nasal spray as well. I was pretty tired all afternoon yesterday and when I got up this morning I was about as tired as I was when I went to bed. I have been told that the radiation will cause quite a bit of fatigue, so I guess we are getting to that stage. I am actually so tired that I dread the drive into the doctor today. Just got off the phone with Dr. Harvey's office. He does want to start weekly chemo tomorrow. It is supposed to be weaker does and hopefully without the nausea. I must go talk to them now after radiation today. This afternoon just gets to sounding better and better! Oh, and each chemo treatment takes 4 hours.

Well, it is Wednesday evening. I had a pretty good day. Radiation went well and I met with nutritionist and doctor. They are going to do two (2) radiation treatments tomorrow and two (2) on next Thursday as well - trying to catch up a bit. Hopefully, the chemo on Monday will not make me sick enough to disrupt the radiation schedule. If everything goes well, by Friday of next week, I will be a little over halfway through the treatments.

Okay. So, the doctor had just asked me yesterday about my throat and, at that time, it was still doing well. But breakfast was a challenge this morning. I cooked my sausage, fried eggs and toast. I had thought that the throat was feeling a bit sore last night, but it was almost impossible to get breakfast down this morning. I will probably get my script for the magic mouthwash today and hope that stuff works well. It may be about time to graduate to smoothies and ice cream and pudding. I meet with the nutritionist tomorrow and I am sure she will have suggestions.

This is a Thursday night update. Today was a long day, and the first time they have done two radiation treatments in the same day. I had the first treatment this morning at 9:15. Then I had to kill some time by going to do some shopping for a new bed. I met my brother for lunch, and we had a rather long, but leisurely lunch. Then, it was time to go back and get blood work done and, as soon as the six (6) hour window was up, they did the second radiation treatment for the day. The bright point in this was that we are now one-third of the way through. The only effects that I am seeing is that this much activity in one day sure tires me out a lot more than it used to. Also, I thought we had the thickened mucus issue handled, but it is quite a bit worse tonight. The throat is still only mildly irritated, but the doctor seems to think it will get much worse soon. She does tend to talk a bit on the pessimistic side though. Again, it is in God's hands and it will be what He wants it and allows it to be. At least, I am still able to eat solid food for the time being and plan to push that as far as possible. Some food tastes as being affected by the radiation. All in all, it was a great day though.

It is now Friday afternoon and has just not been a good day. I had a headache start during the second treatment yesterday but figured it would go away. It did not. I did not sleep well last night mostly due to the thick mucus issue being worse. Today I still had the headache so after getting work done, I took a couple of Tylenols and lay down. I slept for a bit but still had the headache when I woke up. I told the nurse about it when I went for treatment this afternoon and so I had to stay and see the nurse practitioner after treatment. She questioned, said take Tylenol and if that didn't work, go ahead and take oxycodone. She said we must watch for signs of inflammation irritation and that the headache would simply be a sign of that. She did warn me that if a headache started that Tylenol or the oxycodone would not stop to get to the hospital. Apparently, that would be a sign of the inflammation getting around the brain stem, especially if accompanied by nausea. Of course, vision changes would also be an issue. Since I got home and got some food down, the headache seems to have calmed down and almost gone away. So many foods just don't taste good right now, but still eating the ones I can. At least I have a couple of days break from treatment and she said that would give the inflammation time to subside and the irritation calm down. They gave me a prescription for liquid oxycodone and said go ahead and get it filled so that I would have that on hand when throat got too sore to swallow. But, so far, the throat soreness is not bad at all. My voice sounds horribly hoarse, but the soreness is not bad. I am sorry I missed the Happy Hour at Mom's this afternoon. I really wish I had felt like joining the crowd. Maybe next time!!

Even though a few minutes after midnight I thought I would go ahead and do a Saturday update. Thank the Lord I had a good day today. I was able to take mother to Wetumpka today, something I had not been able to do in quite a while. I was able to do this thanks to a couple of very dear men - Bryan and Jason. They were available to go along as spare drivers. Actually, Bryan did most of the driving, but Jason was available in case I had to take meds and needed someone to drive on home once we dropped Bryan. I did have to take a couple of Tylenols for a headache this morning, but it didn't get too bad. My throat is a bit sore, but I was able to eat dinner. However, I am losing my voice it seems, at least for tonight. I don't know how long that will last. Jason - don't get excited. It may come back tomorrow. Once again, I really hope to wake up in the morning feeling like personally attending church. It has been way too long. I am thankful that I can stream services, but I really miss going in person. I am trying not to be apprehensive about doing chemo again after the last two so I am working hard on just trusting this to God along with all the rest of this.

Again, even though after midnight this is Sunday's update. My throat was so sore this morning that I used the miracle mouthwash and apparently it just knocked me out. I didn't wake back up until 12:45. It has just been a restful day. I did get a bit of work done as tomorrow will be so busy and there is a good bit of grading to get done. I also have a class to do tomorrow night and not sure how that is going to work as I have just about lost my voice. But will work it out. I have the anti-nausea patch on and certainly hope that it, together with the steroids in the a.m. and the anti-nausea meds they will give me with the chemo, will keep me from getting sick this time. If I can stay on schedule with the radiation this week, I will be just over halfway through by end of week. So far, I am still able to find solid food I can eat although most of it doesn't taste quite right. I had a grilled hamburger patty with a mix of baked cucumber and squash mixture for dinner. My devotional verse for today was quite uplifting. Mark 11:24:

> *"I tell you, you can pray for anything, and if you believe that you've received it, it will be yours." Mark 11:24*

I do not know God's will in this, but I have trusted this to Him and am willing to accept whatever His will is. Of course, I pray that His healing hand will move in this and it may or may not. But I also pray and believe that whatever the outcome, good will come of this. I appreciate each of you who check in to see how I am doing. I appreciate all the prayers. There is much power in prayer. So, with that I will look toward tomorrow believing that God will be by my side and trust that He will bring me through this next round of chemo unscathed.

Well a late Tuesday night update. They did a chemo treatment

Monday morning and then radiation. I went ahead and took anti-nausea meds Monday night and another this morning. I have been tired today but think it was because everything tasted so bad today, I just couldn't really get food down. For dinner I threw some green beans, onions, potatoes, and smoked sausage in the pressure cooker. Thankfully it tasted good and I ate couple of plates. I didn't exactly jump up and do cartwheels but felt a bit more energetic. I saw Dr Harvey yesterday and saw the radiology oncologist today. It seems they are satisfied so far. She had expected me to be to the oxycodone level of the pain management by now, but I've only had to take Tylenol twice. Of course, I realize that at some point I will have more pain but for this time being I am certain that God is walking right alongside with His arm around my shoulder. I am not yet having to use pain meds and am still able to swallow meds and eat solid food.

Quick Thursday morning update. Had a good day yesterday. Had a not so good night last night though. Up about every 2 hours battling just the dryness in the mouth and throat. Thankfully, there is no throat soreness - I just wake up feeling like my mouth is dry as sand. I am running humidifier in the room 24/7 but may have to go to a second one or at least a larger one. Today is "double treatment" day again - the last one we hope. Thank God I have had no nausea from Monday's chemo so maybe we are going to be successful in doing the weekly chemo treatments now with no nausea to interrupt the radiation schedule. Today will be treatments # 16 and #17. My first treatment is at 9:15 am and then back at 3:15 pm for second one. There must be 6 hours between treatments. There will be 33 total treatments, so today puts me at the halfway mark. Feeling blessed to still not have major sore throat issues and still be able to eat solid food with no swallowing issues. Of course, taste is getting worse - many foods with no taste and many that just taste awful now.

This is a Saturday afternoon update. I had a fair day yesterday, I guess. I got radiation treatment 18 out of the way. Went to Shrimp Basket for dinner and the fish and green beans tasted pretty good. Unfortunately, I didn't keep food with me. The chemo is causing so many digestive issues. It is getting harder and harder to find stuff to eat. Some stuff just has no taste at all, so it is like trying to eat a piece of cardboard. Then some things just simply have such a bad taste that it just gags me. My throat is tolerating the side effects of radiation well so far. Soreness is not an issue. I guess I just must keep trying to find foods that have some degree of decent taste. And it is stuff I normally like that doesn't taste good. Even my strawberries are tasting bad. Grapes and bananas just have no taste. Anybody got suggestions? Don't have a ton of energy today so just resting this afternoon.

It is early Monday morning and I am certainly having to rely on my "go to" verse at this point. I am having major issues finding food that I can eat. My throat is not that sore, but some foods just now taste so bad that I can't get them down. Some just have no taste - like trying to eat cardboard. Funny, but most of the ones that taste so bad are foods I normally love, strawberries, pears, grapes, etc. Also, most of what little food I am being able to get down is just not staying with me. I assume the taste is a combination of the radiation and chemo, but also assume that the chemo is the main reason for the digestive issues. I am really having to fight to remember that God has this, and He is in control. I am very thankful to Him that I am not having a bunch of pain, but it is so easy to get frustrated trying to keep eating even though I know the more solid food I can get down and retain, the better my strength will remain. I can tell I have certainly gotten weaker over the past few days though. Today is another chemo treatment, followed by radiation treatment number 19. At least I am a bit over halfway with the radiation. As far as I know, they have five (5) more chemo treatments scheduled after today (once a week). I am determined to remember to simply rely on God through this. His word promises He will comfort and protect us, so I must hang onto that.

This is a Wednesday afternoon update. Well, I will start by saying that I was very ambitious yesterday. I went and picked mother up and we met my brother for lunch - an experiment - at Golden Corral so I could have a wide variety to choose from and try to find some foods that don't simply taste so bad I can't eat them. I found very few. After lunch Mother and I ran some errands and then it was time to go for radiation. Afterward, of course, I took her back. So, I left home about 10 a.m. and got back close to 7 p.m. I think. It turned out to be a bit too ambitious, so I crashed shortly after I got home. Today was already scheduled to be a busy day, so I haven't felt the best - just mostly really tired. But, I made it to the afternoon doctor's appointment, got radiation treatment number 21 out of the way but then had to stay and meet with nutritionist. Doctor is threatening a PEG line (feeding tube) which, today I said not yet. This was because I had lost 7 pounds in a week. But I think digestive issues last week resulting from the chemo was the culprit there. The nutritionist gave me some ideas - and they want me to shoot for a calorie intake of 1800 calories a day. I don't know that I see that happening, but I am still determined to eat solid foods for as long as I can. The good news is I only have two more weeks of radiation after this weekend. If I can just not lose any more weight, I can probably make it through without the line. Dr. "D" seemed amazed that I was not to the liquid oxy stage of the pain management program, but so far, I haven't started the pain management program. God does provide comfort and strength and I want to take this opportunity to thank everyone for all the encouragement, well wishes and prayers. So, that's all for now. I am going to go crash again. I think I will be able to rest well again tonight. And, regardless of how energetic I think I may be in the morning, I am going to get work stuff done and sit on my behind the rest of the day - except for a quick trip to the grocery store to get some stuff they suggested I try.

Well, it is Saturday morning and it has been a bit since an update. I had radiation treatment number 23 yesterday morning. I have 10 to go - so two more weeks. The issue now is that Dr. "D" threatening a PEG line (feeding tube). It has become almost impossible to find anything that I can stomach putting in my mouth to eat. I am not ready to give up on this, but the platinum-based chemo gives everything such a nasty metal taste. A few things just have no taste, but most just taste bad. The main point now will be to try to get enough nourishment down to make it through the remaining radiation treatments. Unfortunately, there are 6 more weekly rounds of chemo. As for the side effects of the radiation, they have been minimal. My throat is a little sore, but mainly just feels more scratchy than sore. They had predicted that, by the first part of week three, we would be in the narcotic stage of the pain management program, meaning the oxycodone stage. But I have to say, the good Lord is walking through this valley with me. So far, I have not had the need for any pain management. The fatigue from lack of nutrition is certainly showing and I crash rather early most evenings. But I am still determined to continue looking for foods I can get down. At least, I have a couple of days off here from radiation and can try to rest up a bit. Round 3 of weekly chemo will be Monday so no real relief for the taste issue in sight. SIGH!

This is a Monday morning update. It has been a rough weekend. I am not going in for chemo this morning but am instead calling to set an appointment with the doctor. My intention is to at least suspend chemo until these last two weeks of radiation are completed. My body has not dealt well with the chemo from the beginning. I know that I am not a doctor, but I cannot see how not being able to keep any nutrition in my body, and having my body so terribly weak, is doing any good at all. I do not need to lose any more weight until this radiation is done, or it will disrupt the radiation. The nausea is being controlled, but the diarrhea is not. It is a huge struggle just to find something that I can get a few bites of down without gagging. Then, when I do, it goes straight through and that is with me taking medication. This is a result of the chemo - not the radiation. Thank the Lord, I am dealing well with the side effects of the radiation so far. My throat is not sore, no mouth sores, only one tiny skin issue on neck, so all that is getting along well for the moment. I have been told that the radiation is the most important as that is what kills the cancer cells. So, possibly not a popular decision, I do believe that I will opt to suspend the chemo for now. I am pretty sure I will get some guff from the oncologist about this, and possibly both doctors. Guess we will find out today.

Well it is late Monday night. I had a long afternoon at doctors' offices. I had lost 5 more pounds, so I had to talk to Dr. "D", who is my radiation oncologist. I told her that I was meeting with Dr Harvey and that I wanted to at least for the moment suspend the chemo. She absolutely agreed. I then went to meet with Dr Harvey. I told him what I wanted to do, and he said that we were stopping chemo period. He said I would finish radiation and wait for a good scan to see whether any more would be necessary. That was certainly good news for me, and I am wishing we had left it at that. Dr Harvey wanted to try a test dose of a hormone which should wipe out the diarrhea. I agreed and they administered a test dose. It only took about 5 minutes to put me in the restroom with nausea. Eventually that passed and I told them I would not take any more. I came home and went to bed thinking it was over. But I woke up a few minutes ago nauseated and throwing up again. Not that there is much in my system at all. Hopefully this will quickly pass. I do have some Phenergan on board and will take one if the nausea returns. My mission now will be to continue to try to eat and I am hopeful that halting the chemo will soon let my taste return more towards normal so I can start eating again.

Okay, so it is about 1 PM on Wednesday now. Since Monday night, things have not gone well. The "test dose" of the hormone they gave me Monday has really played havoc. I continued to be nauseous throughout the night Monday and all day yesterday. As a result, we were unable to do the radiation treatment yesterday, not to mention that it zapped what little energy I had. As of this morning, stomach seems to be settled. I have been getting down chicken noodle soup and am feeling much better. Since today started the Fall semester at Georgia, I had a class today at 10:00 am, which I did virtually. I got through that successfully and have, in fact, gotten gradebooks set up for all 4 courses, etc. It has been a busy workday so far. And, I have to say, it feels GREAT to be back at work. Thank the Lord for settling the medicine issues and providing strength. Hopefully the side effects of the chemo are about to diminish since I have not had any since Monday of last week. I know that the radiation affects the taste to some degree, but honestly feel that most of the issues with taste and trying to find something I can actually get down has more to do with the chemo. So, hopefully I can expand my diet soon. Thanks to everyone for all the prayers - there is a ton of power in prayer and thanks for checking in on me.

I am sorry I have not updated in a while. It has been a kind of rough few days. I was too sick on Tuesday to have the radiation done, so we doubled up on Thursday. I actually was able to take myself on Thursday morning, but it proved to be a bit too much, so Andy had to take me that afternoon. I am still fighting to maintain weight. It is still a battle to find something I can stomach putting my mouth even but am still trying. Friday was treatment was number 28, so I have 5 more to go. The last treatment will be this coming Friday. Then, we will have to wait 4 to 5 weeks before PET scan can be done. This will probably be a welcome break since there should be no kind of treatment going on. I know that the side effects will probably be slow in dissipating, but hoping my taste starts coming back soon. When it gets back to normal, I may eat everything in sight! So far, I have been able to keep up my work, although it is early in the semester. It does feel good to be back at work though. Some of you may be tired of hearing this, but I will still continue to praise God for keeping His arm around me through all this. I have gone through the side effects of radiation much better than most people. My throat still does not hurt and am not having to take any narcotic pain medicines. Again, thanks for checking on me and thanks for all the prayers.

I was going to update last night but I was just too tired. Yesterday was a long day. I ended up working all day before and after the trip to the doctor. Anyway, Dr. "D" was not happy with me since I lost another 3 pounds over the weekend. She is yelling feeding tube, but I told her I felt that was too invasive with no more treatments than I have left. I am still trying to eat, and I do think my taste is very slowly trying to rebound a bit.

In any case, I was supposed to post and start the countdown yesterday, so I am a few hours late but here goes. As of yesterday---5. Yes-treatment #29 done. Again, thanks for all the support and prayers. One of the verses which has kept me going is Psalm 42:8.

"But each day the Lord pours his unfailing love upon me,
and through each night I sing his songs,
praying to God who gives me life."

So, it is Thursday afternoon and treatment #32 is in the books. I took myself today, but it wore me out. It is such a struggle to eat anything that I hope my taste begins to improve very soon. I think the skin burns will start to recover quickly once tomorrow is over. I am sure the taste and saliva thickness will take a bit longer. Anyway, one more day!

CHAPTER 6

"Awaiting the Verdict"

It is early Monday morning, August 27, 2018 and I wanted to update. I had hoped things would be uphill since my last treatment was out of the way but sadly it isn't. My throat had done well throughout the treatments until this last one. The throat is now extremely sore and mostly now struggling to get down hot tea with honey and a bit of chicken noodle soup. Of course, energy level has taken a huge hit as well. But God has kept His arm around my shoulder throughout this so far and I must trust that He will continue to strengthen me and carry me through. I know that there are many prayers going up on my behalf and that there is a huge amount of power in those prayers. Of course, I must do my part as well. I am very thankful for all the prayers. Energy level down to where I haven't been able to be up and around the last couple of days, so mother came yesterday to help with fixing tea soup etc. She stayed over and will be here with me today. This is a huge help. I was able to do coffee tea and soup yesterday and will push more of the same today. I am also using the magic mouthwash. Some people have commented to me on how well I have gone through these treatments both on Facebook and in person. I just want to say it has not been me. I can't take credit for that. Left on my own I don't think I would have made it. All the credit goes to God. I learned early on in this whole thing - even before the diagnosis and treatment started - that I can't actually do anything on my own - without Him. Thanks again to everyone for all the support and all the prayers.

Well, it is now Saturday, September 8, 2018 and it has been quite some time since I did an update. Not much has changed really. I still cannot get food down and it is to the point of being a real issue. I have lost down to about 139 pounds and I barely have enough energy to wiggle most days. I am still working so that is keeping me somewhat busy. Andy and Deanna got moved out last weekend. Andy is still staying here at night though. We left on the 30th and went up to a cabin in Blue Ridge, Ga. Spent a few days in the peace and quiet. We got back Tuesday, and it was back to work. I have an appointment with Dr. "D" on Monday and I know she is going to insist on a PEG tube. I have still not resolved whether I am going to agree to that. I do not know how long they must stay in once they put one in. I do know that Mother and I are scheduled to leave on October 1st on a cruise and I hate to have to have a PEG tube in while on the trip. But I do have to get some nourishment down so I can regain some energy. My throat is not actually sore, and my taste is somewhat returning, it is just getting food down past the thick mucus in the throat that is the issue. I guess I will just wait and see what happens on Monday. Unless the good Lord directs me differently between now and Monday, I have decided to have the PEG line put in. I am doing all I can do towards eating but it is just not enough. I am down to virtually no energy. Can barely get up out of a chair. I am actually being moved downstairs for my bedroom as I simply don't have the energy to get up and down the stairs any more. I just have no energy left to fight with. I think with more nourishment and energy I will make a much speedier and better recovery. Hopefully this won't be too terribly invasive.

Today is September 11, 2018 and I had a doctor's appointment yesterday. It appears that I have lost another 9 pounds in the past two weeks. I barely have the energy to get around right now. They have scheduled the minor surgery to insert a PEG tube for early Thursday morning. Although I fought this idea tooth and nail from the first time the doctor mentioned it, I just don't have the energy to fight it any longer - or do anything else for that matter. However, the doctor says I should start seeing a difference in my energy level in 24 to 48 hours. So, maybe I can get some energy back and I will continue trying to eat. She also says this thick mucus issue (which is what is keeping me from eating - that and the taste of things) should begin to subside in the next couple of weeks. So - hopefully things will get much better soon! God promises to strengthen - and He has walked with me so far - so I have no doubt that I will be feeling much better very soon.

It is September 13, 2018 and I wanted to give a quick update. The surgery to insert the PEG tube went fine. I am home and doing pretty well although I certainly know there is a hole where they shouldn't be.

It is September 15, 2018 and the infusion pump got hooked up yesterday afternoon. I made it through my first night with the pump just fine. I had two cartons of whatever the stuff is last night. It runs continuously. The home healthcare nurse will be out this morning. I can't really tell much difference yet but maybe after today. Of course, the incision is still quite sore especially if I do something that moves the abdominal wall muscles.

It is now Wednesday so it has been four days. I have been using the feeding pump and picking up a couple of ounces of weight per day. I figure it is time to start trying to find some solid food to eat. Of course, I have no idea where to start. I never know how something is going to taste, although sweets just sound repulsive. I thought last night how good a beef taco salad sounded. Of course, if I had gotten one it might have gagged me as soon as I put a bite in my mouth. It gets so frustrating

- So, do I try previously favorite foods?
- Do I try the last things I was successfully able to eat?
- Do I just go with what sounds good in my mind?
- Suggestions?

This is the report for today - I have been up all day. I have gotten 3 or 4 bites of creamed potatoes down. I tried a bite of Salisbury steak and that was it. It tasted horrible. I didn't gag since I quit before I did. I will try again tomorrow. I got my bandages changed and the incision cleaned. Now I have a fresh bandage on, feeding tube hooked up and have gotten into the right position in bed. Now I am just worn out and it is time to rest.

Now it is Friday, September 21, 2018. First, the nurse will be out. I kind of hate that .... I had planned a full bath for when there are enough people back home this afternoon to help me out of tub! LOL But, the nurse will want to change bandages while she is here this morning. My weight is up to 139.6 this morning. They told me yesterday that it was 137 last Friday when they brought the stuff out and nurse came out to set everything up. So - almost 3 pounds in a week - not too bad.

Thanks for the advice Miss Rhonda. It made no sense from a logical standpoint, but I decided I wanted to try a beef taco salad for dinner last night. That had been sounding good to me for a few days and I was able to get several bites of that down - and it did taste really good. I also, snacked on just a few bites of cheese and crackers. The cheese tasted extra sharp even though it was only medium cheddar. But - hey a couple of bites are better than none. Mother will be back this afternoon and a friend coming over, so my big game plan is to actually sit and relax in nice hot tub bath this afternoon. If necessary, Mother can help me get out of tub, plus I have a stationary walker to help with that. Then, if necessary, Jason can help get me back downstairs. I think I will feel much better. We have been running two cartons of "nutrients" (whatever they are) a day but I am expanding to three today. I typically let two cartons run through during the night while I am sleeping but will add one additional one during the day today. The doctor wants me to expand to 4 or 5 per day. We tried 3 the second day tube was in, but I felt like I was about to blow up! Thanks to everyone for the well wishes and prayers. Now, I just have to stand on what has become my favorite scripture verse ... Isaiah 41:10 which tells us not to be afraid for God is with us - and He has certainly been with me through all this. But it also tells us not to be dismayed. This is a little more difficult as my human nature sure gets impatient to get better. But lastly, it promises that He will strengthen us and protect us. We just have to trust Him and let Him do this on His schedule - not ours.

It is September 25, 2018 and I had a doctor appointment yesterday, so it was time for an update. I am still mainly reliant on the feeding tube. I am not really gaining, but the doctor was happy that I had actually maintained without losing any more weight. I added an extra carton per day starting last night, so I should start feeling better and gaining some weight this week. I do have an appointment with the ENT, Doctor Colvin, today as one ear continues to drain for some reason, and he wants to check it out. The doctor seemed content with progress, skin condition, etc., etc. The "BIG" news I guess from yesterday is that my PET scan will be done on November 20th and later that day I will see the doctor and get the verdict.

Right now, I am still working out some kinks to being able to go on the cruise. I have the doctor's blessings (assuming the ear situation is taken care of), and some minor drainage from the entry point of the feeding tube, but it will still present some challenges. I will be taking myself to Dr. Colvin today and running a couple of errands. This will be my first time driving myself anywhere in I can't remember when. I have to decide if I think I will be able to make a 5-hour drive to Mobile by Monday morning and figure out how to deal with the feeding tube (it is given through an infusion pump so hangs on an IV pole). I do have the use of a walker that I will take to help with any walking on the cruise.

It is September 27, 2018 and I had an appointment with Dr. Colvin on Tuesday. He vacuumed out my head - ears and nasal passages. He put me on some antibiotic drops for the right ear to try to clear it up. I will go back to let him recheck it on the 11th. Over the past couple of days, I have gotten down a few bites of solid food. Yesterday I got down most of a Carnation instant breakfast. This morning after nurse left, I thought I would do another one. Yesterday it tasted fine but this morning it tasted so sweet it was gagging me. I got aggravated and simply got the big syringe and put it in slowly via the feeding tube. I reckon because I got aggravated, I was determined that it was going one way or another. I am going to try to eat a bit more tonight. I am frustrated to say the least. It seems we are back to the trying to find something that doesn't taste so bad it gags me. I cooked large lima beans and fried salmon patties - some of my favorite foods. The smell while cooking the salmon was sickening. I ended up eating a very little bit of Jello salad. I didn't even try anything else

Well it is now September 28, 2018 and, even though I have not lost any more weight, I am not making any progress towards eating solid food either. So, my energy level is just not increasing. I got out today and got a couple of errands done, but that little bit really wiped me out. It is looking like Mother may have to miss her "Birthday Cruise". I am just not sure I can get us down there. I did talk to Carnival today and they are willing to be extra accommodating on-board. I am just not sure I can drive us down there. But kudos to Carnival for their help!! I am still working on trying to get solid food down and haven't given up. I just wish my taste would straighten up a bit. And this awful mucus in my throat can go away any time it pleases now! After using the drops the ENT wanted me to use on that right ear, I started itching all over. I have stopped the drops as that is one of the listed possible side effects and it seems to be subsiding a bit. The ear is also doing better, so maybe it will clear up soon. The nurse had been concerned about some discharge from the feeding tube, but that too, seems to be getting better. Thank the good Lord for walking through this with me and keeping His arm around my shoulder. I continue to pray that He will continue to strengthen me and get me back on the road to recovery soon. No way could I have done this without Him.

Well, it is now October 9, 2018 and it has been quite some time since I have done an update. It has been a rough couple of weeks. My energy levels have just bottomed out. Then I started itching. I had to be taken to Mobile for mother's birthday cruise. We were taken on Sunday and dropped off at motel. I ate a few bites on Sunday but was itching all over. I didn't use feeding tube Sunday night. Monday, I was still itching so called my doctor before actually boarding the ship. She said could be thyroid levels since I had forgotten to take m thyroid meds for few days. She old me to take Benadryl which makes me sleepy. I got on ship. Well, I was actually taken on ship in wheelchair. Again, I didn't use feeding tube Monday night. I was simply too tired to fool with it. On Tuesday morning, the itching was better. I didn't get any food down Tuesday so I started to use feeding tube Tuesday evening. In just a few minutes I was itching all over again and within just a few minutes I was in bathroom throwing the stuff up. I said no more of that stuff. Wednesday, I managed to get a few bites down but not much. Thursday the itching was a bit better, but I still wasn't able to get much down. I just didn't even have enough energy to navigate around the ship. Friday was the same. Saturday we were picked up and taken to the cabin in North Carolina. We stopped at a Waffle House and I was able to eat several bites of food. I got some much-needed rest and was able to start eating. By Monday I was able to get around without the walker and the itching is completely gone. I can't eat much at once but will try to eat every few hours. Thank the Lord things are looking up.

It is now October 13, 2018. Saturday morning, so I have been home now for 3 full days. I am feeling fair - not great - but certainly better than I have in the past. I am eating solid food - although I still can't eat but a few bites at a time. I still don't have the energy or strength to tackle the stairs in the house, so I am still stationed in the downstairs makeshift bedroom. The home health care nurse was out yesterday. My vitals were good and she said I looked better. I know I probably lost more weight during the whole complication issue with the feeding tube stuff, but I am back to 135 and seem to be gaining about 2 ounces a day right now. I have not been doing so good on eating every two to three hours but I will work on that. I am working on making all the morning things I am supposed to do a routine. I have also been falling short on getting all those things done before I jump in to work. I guess I am going to have to make a checklist and post on the computer screen and leave it there until I check off all the boxes. At least that way, I can't start work until those are all done. Thanks again for everyone's support through all this. Now, on November 19th they will do the PET scan and I will get the report on November 20th - either I will be cancer free or not! That is totally in the Lord's hands.

Well it is October 16, 2018, Tuesday evening. I have had a setback on eating. I woke up yesterday morning with what seems to have been a 24-hour stomach bug. It sure wiped out what energy I had built up. It seems to also have set back my eating. I have tried to eat three times today unsuccessfully. I will continue working on that though and get back to where I was. I did make it to the ball game last night to watch AJ play. I have been trying to make it to a game all season. I posted a picture of me and him on my timeline on Facebook. He looks so much bigger than me, but I realized there had not been a picture of me taken since I had gotten sick. So, I had a picture taken this afternoon and I have to say I was a little surprised. Thanks again for all the support and prayers.

It is October 27, 2018 I know it is past time for an update. And I wish I had great, glorious news. But - I don't. My last update was October 16th and it has been a continuous fight ever since the stomach bug to start eating again. I have used Boost in the PEG tube, but honestly, I cannot tell any difference in energy doing that. I have been able to eat a few bites - very few - here and there. But, even so, I have lost down to 129 pounds. This past Sunday, the family went to Stix for the oldest grandson's birthday dinner and I ate a ton of food - well a ton for me! I love the ginger salad and I loved the vegetables. But since then, not much luck. I ate some bananas and peanut butter one night. Peanut butter tastes good again, but it is a little hard to get down. I had a terrible morning this morning getting my throat cleared out. It actually took two gagging fits to get it done. I had bought some cabbage, zucchini, yellow squash, water chestnuts and mushrooms. I cut some up and sautéed them in a wok. I put in soy sauce of course, but then I decided to put in some teriyaki and that was a mistake. I could not get it down. I tried to force the second bite down and gagged myself. So, I just did a Boost instead. I am not giving up though - I am going to do some more vegetables tomorrow and only use the soy sauce. I think I will throw in some chicken as well. Hopefully that will go down well. It sounds good to me. If I have the energy tomorrow, I may even go over to Stix and get a ginger salad.

Well, I did go to Georgia this last week. I left on Monday and came home Wednesday evening. It felt good to be back in my office, but it sure took all the energy I had. Mother went with me just in case. I did get some whole kernel corn and crowder peas down a couple of nights over there. Hopefully, the eating issue will improve soon. I am just putting it in God's hands and trying to keep my impatience and my hands off it!!

Well, it is Saturday, November 3rd and well past time for an update. Again, I wish I had better news to report. I am down to 125.4 pounds. Still greatly struggling with eating solid food. It is very frustrating as I had gotten to eating pretty good before the stomach virus. It is like it set me back to square one! But at least I can get up my stairs - maybe only once or twice a day - but new furniture came this morning and I plan to move back up to my own bedroom today. Mother is going to stay another week or so though. I am still working on the eating and using Boost through the PEG tube to help. I am still able to work, have to be in Georgia this next week, and will be leaving Tuesday. Mother will again go with me on the trip. We will be back Friday night. We leave Saturday for another "cabin" trip. We got a house (not really a cabin) in mountains of North Georgia and if I can start eating on this trip like I was able to on the last one, that would be great, grand and wonderful. We don't have a bunch of activity planned - just rest and relax and enjoy the foliage up there and the big fireplace in the house. A friend is going with us and will do the driving. There is also an outside fire pit we can enjoy if it isn't too terribly cold. I still stay cold all the time. Hopefully, I will have better news in a week or so. I am tired of losing weight. I know God has this and I am just letting my impatience get in the way - but it can be hard to be patient.

It is Thursday night, November 18th and I know I have not updated in a while now. Several things have been going on. I am still not eating very well. I can usually get down a few bites of something at least once a day and am using Boost twice a day on most days. I did manage to go to Georgia for work for a week. When we got back, we went to the mountains for just a relaxing time. It was a nice trip and a nice break. Well, tomorrow they are doing my PET scan. Of course, they are going to probably fuss about the weight loss. They were fussing even when I was still up to 135 so I am sure they will not be happy with 124. However, it will be Monday afternoon before I see the doctor and get the actual report. I am really trying not to worry about it - and that is going pretty well. I have felt from the beginning that God's got this. But I do realize that if I am going to trust this to Him, I must be willing to accept whatever His will is in this matter. That gets to be the hard part. Well, it is late, so I better take me up the stairs (yes, I am able to get up my stairs once again) and put me to bed. I am really enjoying my new bed and the recent travels have proven what I suspected the first couple of times I slept on the new bed - IT HELPS! Being able to sleep at an incline (the bed is adjustable), my throat is not as "stopped up" in the mornings. I guess it helps the junk drain! I will post again once I get the report from the doctor on Monday though. Thanks again for all the prayers and support!

It is now November 19, 2018 and the results are in - however, they are not conclusive. There is, in the doctor's words, a small residual area at the back of the nasal cavity that is lighting up on the PET scan. This could be either residual cancer cells or simply inflammation. Given that my right ear is still "running", that indicates there is still inflammation in all that area burnt by the radiation so it is very likely that it could be inflammation. The ENT will scope my head next week and, if he can't tell with certainty, he will do biopsies to make sure which this is. So, while not a conclusive report, it was still a good report.

It is now November 27, 2018 and the trip to Dr. Colvin is done. He had to vacuum and unstop both ears. I can hear again. He had to vacuum head to be able to see anything. He scoped and vacuumed until I started bleeding. He says he sees no sign of a tumor. He did say he could see why I can't eat. Tissue in head is still so burnt and irritated and there is so much mucus. He says he will do more vacuuming while I am asleep for the biopsies. The biopsies will be done on December 5th and they will wait for preliminary results while I am asleep. Today was painful overall but very encouraging. I can see where with so much irritation in the head that there would certainly be inflammation. However, I still have to simply trust God with all this.

It is December 4, 2018 and it has been a few days since I updated, but really nothing to report. I am just waiting on tomorrow. The hospital called and I am scheduled to be there at 7:30 in the morning. Dr. Colvin said I might be there awhile as he is sending biopsies to the Lab and waiting on results. So hopefully I will know tomorrow whether the area still lighting up on the PET scan is residual cancer cells or just inflammation. I vote for inflammation personally. But God's got this. The results will be according to His plan. I will take this opportunity to brag a bit. I have gained 8 ounces each of the past two days. I have really cut back on activity until I can start getting more calories down. I will post what I find out tomorrow or Thursday.

It is December 5, 2018 and I am home from the hospital. I have been there since 7:45 this morning. Dr. Colvin told Andy that he saw nothing discouraging - there was scabbing, and he had to get biopsies from under scab tissue so as not to end up with "dead" tissue. He took a sufficient number of biopsies. He did not see any cancer cells in what he looked at today. Of course, these tissue samples will be analyzed, cultured, or whatever they do by the lab and report in a few days. I believe he also did some additional cleaning on my head and throat as I was able to eat a good portion of a blueberry muffin with my cup of coffee in recovery. I will post updates as I get them. But, right now, I am feeling pretty good.

It is now December 7, 2018. Let me begin by saying this has been one more journey! And, God has been there with me every step of the way! I got a call from the doctor's office ... the reports are in on the biopsies. I am now cancer free! Praise the Lord! I want to thank everyone for their support through this and for all the prayers. Of course, the doctor will continue to monitor closely, but that is to be expected. I am slowly gaining weight back and energy levels are coming up as well. Of course, I am improving as far as eating - but that is still going a bit slowly. There is still quite a bit of mucus and it is still thick. But, as the tissues in the head heal, I am sure that will improve. The ENT says there is quite a bit of scabbing and that things are healing but that it just takes time.

EPILOGUE

"What's Next"

This has certainly been a journey. A journey not planned, wanted, nor prepared for. Nonetheless, a journey with a very strong and important lesson – a journey which resulted in some serious self-examination and the resulting personal revelations.

Self-examination revealed that I was much too self-sufficient – convinced that I could handle and fix anything that came along. Way too much of ME – and not nearly enough of GOD. I'm not saying that God "gives" anyone cancer, but we do live in a fallen and imperfect world of our own making. After all, it was we humans who introduced sin into this world. However, God may choose to "allow" us to go through certain trials. Certainly, this trial held come important lessons for me should I chose to learn them.

First, the self-examination made it very plain that I was not the all-powerful person I though myself to be. Secondly, once I realized this, the question became, "so if I can'[t do it myself, where do I turn?" Sure, I had good doctors, but they are simply humans and I am only one of many patients. No – God was the obvious answer. He actually is all-powerful, and I am not a patient to Him – I am His child. Please don't misunderstand – I had wonderful doctors.

So, once I cam to this realization, I made the choice to trust this situation – this journey, as well as my entire life to God.

Reading the Bible because a daily habit and I leaned that trusting something to God also means being willing to accept His will for the situation. Once I was able to truly trust this trial to God, I had peace with it.

Now, even though my pathology reports were clear, please do not assume that this journey is complete. It most certainly is not. Perhaps, the first part of the journey is over – ended with the pathology reports.

However, the journey now takes a new turn. Still unplanned or unwanted, it now appears that there is a whole new journey to be made – and one with new revelations and lessons. I look forward to bringing those revelations and lessons to you once the journey is complete.

CPSIA information can be obtained
at www.ICGtesting.com
Printed in the USA
BVHW030923120919
558270BV00005B/56/P